Got Got Need

The Beginner's Guide to Sorare

By
Daniel Higgs

Got Got Need by Daniel Higgs

ISBN: **9798704768401**

Got Got Need by Daniel Higgs

TABLE OF CONTENTS

Got Got Need by Daniel Higgs

Got Got Need by Daniel Higgs

AKNOWLEDGMENTS

Firstly, thanks to Sorare for creating this amazing game that is now my obsession.

Thanks to Alex (alexvissaridis.work) for the cover art – see you at the SO5s?!

Cheers to all the Sorare Dorks for the worldwide wisdom, tips and laughs.

Thanks to HG at SorareData (www.soraredata.com) for the resources he provides us all and letting me refer to it throughout the book.

Got Got Need by Daniel Higgs

DISCLAIMERS

Got Got Need by Daniel Higgs

INTRODUCTION

Firstly, many thanks for buying the book, the fact you've made this purchase means you're considering or have already began your journey into the world of Sorare – I am very excited for you.

When I first stumbled across Sorare its fair to say I was a little sceptical, the idea of people collecting digital cards which they couldn't physically hold was a difficult concept to grasp and I gave it a pass. It was a few months later whilst trawling the internet going down the inevitable rabbit holes that we find ourselves falling that I once again crossed paths with Sorare and this time I gave it a bit more time; I dug into what gave the cards value and understanding the game itself then I tried my best to pick holes in the platform's model and I struggled, at this point I was hooked.

Before jumping headfirst into the game, I wanted to understand every aspect of the Sorare world, there are numerous resources scattered across the internet and I found the community to be engaging, informed and very helpful but there was a lot to take in.

In this book I've put all the information I accumulated together to help guide you through each stage of getting started on the platform. Understanding the many aspects of the game can be daunting at first, you'll come across words such as ETH, Blockchain, XP, SO5 – what do they mean? Well, over the course of the next few chapters we'll break it all down and make sure you enjoy the game to its full capacity and hopefully collect some prizes along the way!

From my personal experience I would urge you to read this book and do as much research as possible before even hitting that sign up button; there are some tips and hints here that will set you off on the right foot and ensure you make the most of the game from the start avoiding any newbie mistakes that you will regret further down the line. There is also a useful sign-up code that will give you an extra 100M to spend on your first Sorare team plus a free rare card!

Let's get going…

Got Got Need by Daniel Higgs

<u>1</u>
WHAT IS SORARE?

Sorare is a fantasy football game played with digital collectible cards that each represent a real football player; there are numerous weekly tournaments which can be entered to compete for prizes of Ether/ Eth or other collectible cards.

Ether/ Eth
This is a digital currency usually referred to as cryptocurrency; you may have heard of Bitcoin, well it's very similar to that. ETH is supported on the Ethereum blockchain, a secure network of data. Everything that happens on Sorare is recorded and stored on the Ethereum blockchain – do not worry yourself if this all sounds technical, it will not greatly affect your user experience on Sorare. As with traditional money (often referred to as fiat), ETH can be traded back to other currencies such as £, € and $, we will get more into how this is done later in the book. You can see how much ETH is currently worth by visiting this link: <u>https://coinmarketcap.com/converter/eth/gbp/</u>

Each Sorare card has a limited supply (you will see people refer to this as scarcity). Every season a player will have 111 cards produced, these will consist of three levels: 'Rare' (100 cards), 'Super Rare' (10 cards) and 'Unique' (1 card). Cards are used to play the game; they are yours forever unless you choose to sell or trade them with another collector.

NFT/ Non-fungible Token
You may see Sorare cards described sometimes as NFTs or Non-fungible token; these take many forms but in the simplest terms are unique and rare digital assets – a website domain name could be described as an NFT but there's also digital art and in-game collectibles to name just a few. Anything that is desirable and hard to come by will always have a market sometimes commanding a huge amount of money. If you would like to find out more here's an in-depth guide to NFTs: <u>https://cointelegraph.com/magazine/nonfungible-tokens/#/</u>

Got Got Need by Daniel Higgs

UNDERSTANDING THE GAME

2
UNDERSTANDING THE GAME

I know you'll be really eager to get going but I do strongly suggest that you familiarise yourself with how the game works before you even think of skipping to the sign-up walkthrough section of this book, not only is there a nice little bonus link in here that will give you an extra 100M to spend on your first players and a free Rare card but if you can understand what gives the cards their value and how the tournament structures work you'll be able to build a successful team much more efficiently, so please have a read through of the following sections beforehand.

In essence the game is as simple as collecting and choosing a team of 5 player cards then putting them up against other people's team selections, the winners are those who score the most points.

Cards are either obtained by winning tournaments or buying/ trading them via the Market.

The game itself is called Sorare5 or SO5 for short (the 5 referring to the number of player cards). Twice a week there are a selection of tournaments that can be entered for free, the 2 sessions or 'game weeks' are 1) Fridays 17.00 ending Tuesday at 05.00 and 2) Tuesdays 17.00 ending Fridays at 05.00

You are the manager and must pick a team of 5 consisting of the following: -

- 1 x Goalkeeper
- 1 x Defender
- 1 x Midfielder
- 1 x Attacker
- 1 x Extra Outfield Player

Only one of each player can be selected for your team, for example you cannot have 2 x Cristiano Ronaldo in your side. You must also allocate the team captaincy to one of your players, whoever you select as your captain will receive a power boost.

Got Got Need by Daniel Higgs

<u>3</u>
THE SCORING SYSTEM

If you've had any previous experience of playing Fantasy Football or other games such as Football Index or Footstock you should be able to grasp the mechanics of the Sorare scoring system quite easily. Try not to feel overwhelmed reading through this section, there is a lot to take in but as you start playing the game it will become clear and Sorare do a good job of making things as simple as possible when it comes to presenting the info you need on gamedays.

Understanding how the cards score is vital, 'Points mean Prizes!'. Apart from some very exceptional circumstances (that we will look at in Chapter 10) the value of a card is determined by its ability to earn a team points.

A team's total score is calculated by adding all 5 of your card scores together; card scores are worked out using the following calculation:

Card Score = Player Score x (1 + Bonus Score)

1) Player Score – Calculated using the scoring matrix. Points are attributed based upon the players performance in game and taken from Opta database.
2) Bonus Score – Calculated using each card's bonus attributes.

Opta

Generally regarded as the world leading supplier of detailed sports data. The company collects and analyses data from many different sporting events then distributes it to a vast range of clients including broadcasters, betting companies and football teams. Sorare draws all their in-game stats from the Opta database meaning that your player cards can continue to score gameweek points even if they were to move to one of the other global leagues.
You can read more about the Opta Football here https://www.optasports.com/sports/football/
You can see which leagues Sorare currently cover here https://sorare.com/faq?selection=Coverage

1) <u>Player Score (PS)</u>

Player scores range from 0 (terrible performance or 'Did Not Play') to 100 (man of the match stuff). You will see on Mbappe's page below the score from his last 5 games, DNP stands for 'Did Not Play':

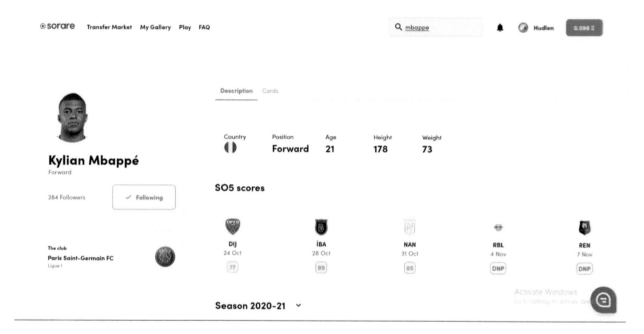

Player Score is calculated using the following formula:

Player Score = Decisive Score + All-around Score

<u>Decisive Score</u>

Based on stats that have a direct and significant positive or negative impact on the game such as a goal, assist or red card (see chart opposite).

POSITIVE IMPACT	NEGATIVE IMPACT
GOAL	RED CARD
ASSIST	OWN GOAL
PENALTY WON	PENALTY CONCEDED
CLEARANCE OFF THE LINE	ERROR LEADS TO GOAL
CLEANSHEET (ONLY GK)	CONCEDE 3 OR MORE GOALS (GK ONLY)
PENALTY SAVE	
LAST MAN TACKLE	

The Decisive Score is calculated using the grid below; a player will start at level 0, if they are in the starting 11 they will get 35 points, if they are a substitute, they will get 25 points. Every time the player makes a positive impact within the game the player will go up a level, if they make a negative impact they go down. Levels over 0 will guarantee the player a score after the final whistle i.e. the score cannot be lower than this regardless of the All-around Score:

LEVEL	POINTS	GUARANTEED
-1	15	NO
0	35	NO
1	60	YES
2	70	YES
3	80	YES
4	90	YES
5	100	YES

Example 1: Robert Lewandowski scores a hattrick (up 3 levels) but receives a yellow card (down 1 level) so ends up on Level 2 @ 70 Points.

Example 2: Alex Sandro concedes a penalty (down 1 level) and is given a red card (down 1 level but already below 0) so ends up on Level -1 @ 15 Points.

All-around Score

Formed from a multitude of other stats tracked during the progress of the game from the grid on pages 10 and 11. The total is then added to the 'Decisive Score' to give you the total 'Player Score'.

CATEGORY	STAT	GK	DEF	MID	FWD
GENERAL	YELLOW CARD	-3.0	-3.0	-3.0	-3.0
GENERAL	FOULS		-1.0	-0.5	
GENERAL	WAS FOULED			0.5	1.0
GENERAL	ERROR LEADS TO SHOT	-5.0	-1.0	-1.0	-1.0
DEFENDING	CLEAN SHEET		10.0		
DEFENDING	GOALS CONCEDED		-0.2	-2.0	
DEFENDING	EFFECTIVE CLEARANCE		0.5		
DEFENDING	WON TACKLE		3.0	3.0	
DEFENDING	BLOCKED CROSS		1.0	1.0	
DEFENDING	BLOCK		2.0	1.0	
DEFENDING	DOUBLE DOUBLE		4.0	4.0	4.0
DEFENDING	TRIPLE DOUBLE		6.0	6.0	6.0
DEFENDING	TRIPLE TRIPLE		12.0	12.0	12.0
POSSESION	POSSESION LOST	-0.3	-1.0	-0.5	-0.1
POSSESION	POSSESION WON		0.5	0.5	
POSSESION	DUEL LOST		-2.0	-0.5	-0.5
POSSESION	DUEL WON		1.5	0.5	0.5
POSSESION	INTERCEPTION		3.0	2.0	

CATEGORY	STAT	GK	DEF	MID	FWD
PASSING	BIG CHANCE CREATED	3.0	3.0	3.0	3.0
PASSING	ATTEMPTED ASSIST	2.0	2.0	2.0	2.0
PASSING	ACCURATE PASS		0.1	0.1	0.1
PASSING	ACCURATE FINAL 3RD PASS		0.5	0.3	0.1
PASSING	ACCURATE LONG BALL	0.2	0.5	0.5	
PASSING	LONG PASS INTO OPPOSITION		0.5		
PASSING	MISSED PASS		-0.2	-0.2	
ATTACKING	SHOT ON TARGET	3.0	3.0	3.0	3.0
ATTACKING	WON CONTEST		0.5	0.5	0.5
ATTACKING	PENALTY AREA ENTRY		0.5	0.5	0.5
ATTACKING	PENALTY KICK MISSED	-5.0	-5.0	-5.0	-5.0
ATTACKING	BIG CHANCE MISSED	-5.0	-5.0	-5.0	-5.0
GOALKEEPING	SAVED SHOT FROM INSIDE BOX	1.0			
GOALKEEPING	GOOD HIGH CLAIM	1.2			
GOALKEEPING	PUNCH	1.2			
GOALKEEPING	DIVING SAVE	3.0			
GOALKEEPING	DIVING CATCH	3.5			
GOALKEEPING	CROSS NOT CLAIMED	-5.0			
GOALKEEPING	SIX SECOND VIOLATION	-5.0			
GOALKEEPING	GK SMOTHER	5.0			
GOALKEEPING	KEEPER SWEEPER	5.0			

You will notice by the scoring system that it's desirable to have players that are heavily involved in games in a positive manner – plenty of touches, passes, saves, tackles, shots etc – if they get goals or assists even better, keep this in mind and begin making a list of some players that you feel will score highly.

Double Double? Triple Triple?

One of the most common questions when assessing the scoring matrix is what is meant by double double, triple double and triple triple. Simply put:

Double Double: 2 of any 2 of the following – interceptions, won tackles and duels (*net amount*)
Triple Double: 3 of any 2 of the following – interceptions, won tackles and duels (*net amount*)
Triple Triple: 3 of any 3 of the following – interceptions, won tackles and duels (*net amount*)

2) Bonus Score

Cards have 3 types of bonus that can be applied:

- Captain bonus @ 20% (This is for the card you allocated as your team captain)
- Season bonus @ 5% (This is if your card is from the current football season)
- Level bonus – this will depend on the XP (Experience Points) your card has and what scarcity it is

XP

Each time a card is used in a tournament it will gain XP and this in turn will level up the card. Each time a card levels up it will gain 0.5% of bonus. 20 levels are the maximum a card can level up. In general, a card should if being used regularly, go up 10 levels in year 1 and further 10 over the next 2 years. The table opposite shows the progression of levels as your card earns XP.

The XP level a card starts on is dependent on its scarcity:
- Rare – Start at Level 0 – can reach a maximum level of 20; level bonus range from 0 to 10%
- Super Rare – Start at Level 40 – can reach a maximum level of 60; level bonus from 20% to 30%
- Uniques – Start at Level 80 – can reach a maximum level of 100; level bonus from 40% to 50%

XP	LEVEL
0	1
100	2
300	3
600	4
1,000	5
1,500	6
2,100	7
2,800	8
3,600	9
4,500	10
5,500	11
6,600	12
7,800	13
9,100	14
10,500	15
12,000	16
13,600	17
15,300	18
17,100	19
19,000	20
21,000	21

XP Progression Chart

Let's have a look at some card's profiles and their level bonus:

+8%

Neymar [Rare]. 2020-21 Season, the current season at time of writing so this card will receive a +5% Season Bonus. Below the card you will see '+8%', this shows the Bonus Level of this particular card; so we can assume this card will be a Level 6 (6 x 0.5 = 3% + 5% Season Bonus = 8%). Later in the book we will take a closer look at all the information on these cards and their profiles.

+25.5% 23

João Félix [Super Rare]. 2019-20 Season, not the current season so no Season Bonus. Bonus Level +25.5% so this card will be a Level 51 (51 x 0.5 = 25.5%).

+46.5%

Cristiano Ronaldo [Ultra Rare]. 2019-20 season so no Season Bonus. Bonus Level us +46.5% so this will be a Level 93.

So, we have looked at how the cards score points, why some cards have more power than others and we've started to consider the kind of players we may want to target for our squad. The next step is to assess the tournaments we can enter our teams into so that we can build a squad that has the right attributes to be successful.

Got Got Need by Daniel Higgs

5

THE SO5 TOURNAMENTS

There are a range of tournaments to enter each gameweek; each tournament has its own criteria in order for a team to enter:

Starter League Rookie: Free to play division for new users only for their first 8 weeks on the platform. Team must consist of Commons cards and up to a maximum of 2 Rares only.

The Global Structure: These leagues can be played with any players from any combination of leagues e.g. goalkeeper from Asia, defender and midfielder from Europe and forward from America:

- **All Star League**: Divisions 1-4
- **Under 23 League**: Divisions 1-4, players must be 23 or under as of July 1ˢᵗ of the current year
- **Unique**: 1 Division, all players must be uniques

The Regional Structures:

- **European Champions League**: Divisions 1-4. Players must play in the top 5 European football leagues: Premier League, La Liga, Serie A, Bundesliga, Ligue 1.
- **American Champions League**: Divisions 1-4. Players must play in the American leagues currently covered in Sorare: MLS, Superliga Argentina, Liga MX, Colombian Primera A, Brasileiro Serie A.
- **Asian Champions League**: Divisions 1-4. Players must play in the Asian leagues currently covered in Sorare: J.League, K League, Chinese Super League.
- **European Challenger League**: Divisions 1-4. Players must play in all other European Leagues outside the top 5 European leagues currently covered in Sorare: Portuguese Liga, Russian Premier League, Eredivisie, Belgium Pro League, Scottish Premiership, Turkish SuperLig, English Championship.

The Special Structures:

- **Training League**: Not a league as such but you can enter a team of any players from a combination of leagues and scarcity levels (Unique, Super Rare, Rare and Common). There are no prizes to be won but players XP does increase each time they play.
- **Weekly Challenge**: In order to enter Sorare's weekly challenge your team will need to meet a certain criteria set by them e.g. all players must be over 33 years old/ only players from Ligue 1. Can be played with any combination of cards (Unique, Super Rare and Rare).

Each division in each league has criteria set for the level of cards you can enter based on their strength, for example Division 4 teams must have at least 4 Rares with the 5th position either being a Rare or Common, the table below shows what you need in each division:

LEAGUE	D4	D3	D2	D1
Playable Cards	At least: 4 Rares	At least: 3 Rares	At least: 3 Super Rares	At least: 3 Uniques
	Fillable with: 1 Common	Fillable with: Super Rare	Fillable with: Max 1 Unique Max 1 Rare	Fillable with: Super Rares
	Captain: Rare	Captain: Rare	Captain: Super Rare	Captain: Unique

You must own all player cards that you select at the gameweek deadline. As soon as the deadline passes, you are then free to sell your cards on the market but still claim their points that gameweek.

The Prizes

Each tournament has an allocated set of prizes which varies each week; most week's prizes range from cards and/ or Eth, as you climb the divisions the prizes get bigger and more desirable i.e. premium cards and more Eth. Later in the book we will look where you can find prize information and see how it can help in your squad building decisions.

The last thing we are going to look at before we start building our team is the data resources available to help inform your initial squad picks then when you get buying and selling on the marketplaces.

Got Got Need by Daniel Higgs

<u>6</u>
THE DATA

So, we now know that a player card has value in its ability to earn points, but how can we find out the historical data/ past scores of a card and how can we use that information to decide on which players to go for in our squad?

We are lucky enough with Sorare that it has a 3rd party site that is both incredibly useful and, at present, absolutely free to use - <u>SorareData</u>. I would go as far to say that you need to use this website if you are going to have long term success in the game so your first job at this stage is to go to <u>www.soraredata.com</u> and bookmark it in your favourites.

SorareData uses the data from the Ethereum blockchain, which Sorare runs on, as well as shared data that is put out on a public API (Application Public Interface).

There is a wealth of information on the website and as you get to grips with the many aspects of the game you will find a use for each of the features. The website can be linked to your Sorare profile and this will enable data to be cross-integrated allowing you to view information about your squad and help make decisions on tournament entries. The website is also vital in forming valuations as you begin to get to grips with the transfer market, we will begin to look at this in more detail as we check out the website's great features.

It may seem odd to you at this stage that we are checking out a 3rd party website before we have even signed up to Sorare yet but there is a reason for this – the data that this website gives will help to inform your decisions when putting together your Rookie team when you sign up, this is giving you an edge!

Home Screen

Below is the home screen you are greeted with when you access the website:

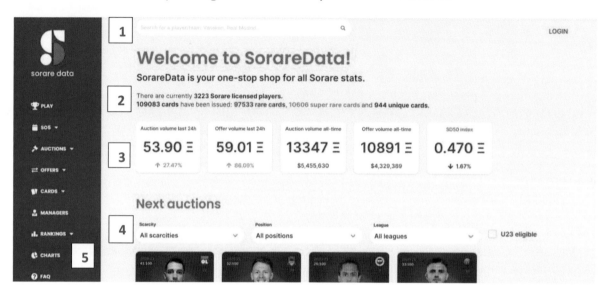

1) Search Bar – From here type in any players name and if they are on the Sorare platform you will be able to see all their data information.
2) Sorare Card Summary – Shows how many players are licensed on the platform available as cards and then breaks down exactly how many cards have been issued.
3) Auction Summary – Shows the volume of action with auctions and offers within the stated 24 hours and all-time. The SD50 index represents the monthly average rare card price of the top 50 players on Sorare; this is a fair indicator of how the Sorare market is performing – it would be reasonable to assume that if prices are on the rise that new users are joining the platform and driving prices up, if the average rare card price is dropping this could indicate a drop in sentiment.
4) Next Auctions – Scroll down here and you will be able to view all the latest cards up for auction similar to the Sorare site itself but with some handy at-a-glance information such as 1 month average price and best market price.
5) Menu Bar – From here you can navigate around the many features of Soraredata including being able to search all other managers on the platform and looking at present or past S05 tournament data.

Player Profile

Probably the most used feature of Soraredata is viewing player profiles and their respective data; try typing any players name into the search bar and if the player is on Sorare you will bring up a screen that looks like this:

1) Players name (Nikola Vlasic)
2) Position (Mid/ Midfielder) [Other positions are GK/Goalkeeper, Def/Defender & Fwd/Forward]

   Playing status (Tick indicates no known injury or suspension) [An X would mean that they are either unlikely to play the next game or not in an Opta covered league)

   N.B always do your own research – this data is only as good as the source, I see quite regularly players with an X against their name but are then in the starting 11, check as many reliable sources as possible – Fotmob, Whoscored, Sofascore, Flashscores along with twitter feeds all can be checked to see the latest team news

   Ranking among same position (ranked 15th) and ranking among all players (ranked 34th)

   Number of cards in existence (86 Rares, 19 Super Rares, 2 Uniques)

3) Age (23)

Current club (CSKA)

Player status based on last 5 games (Starter) [Other statuses are Substitute or Reserve]

4) Average scores and number of games in starting 11 over defined period (Average score is 70 in last 5 games, started 80% of games/ 65 in last 15, started 93%/ 65 in last 40, started 93%)

5) Average Eth price of cards sold over defined periods and the current best market offer available (Rare 0.795 Eth, best market offer 0.700 Eth/ Super rare 3.240 Eth, best market offer 6.600 Eth/ Unique 16.380 Eth, no market offers)

6) States if you own any cards of this player

Scroll down the screen and you will have further options for looking more in depth at some select data:

Selling ranges

	Selling ranges	Price history	Offers	Auctions	SO5 Scores
3 days	**0.700 Ξ** No auction 1 offer: 0.700 Ξ		**3.146 Ξ** 1 auction: 3.146 Ξ No offer		**No sale** No auction No offer
15 days	**0.700 - 0.918 Ξ** 2 auctions: 0.733 - 0.918 Ξ 3 offers: 0.700 - 0.900 Ξ		**3.146 Ξ** 1 auction: 3.146 Ξ No offer		**No sale** No auction No offer
30 days	**0.700 - 1.033 Ξ** 6 auctions: 0.733 - 1.033 Ξ 5 offers: 0.700 - 0.990 Ξ		**3.146 Ξ** 1 auction: 3.146 Ξ No offer		**No sale** No auction No offer
All-time	**0.218 - 1.185 Ξ** 52 auctions: 0.218 - 1.033 Ξ 23 offers: 0.275 - 1.185 Ξ		**1.210 - 5.800 Ξ** 6 auctions: 1.210 - 3.315 Ξ 5 offers: 1.750 - 5.800 Ξ		**11.312 - 16.380 Ξ** 2 auctions: 11.312 - 16.380 Ξ No offer

From here we can see the selling price ranges from the time durations noted in the primary (auctions) and secondary (offers/ manager to manager) markets. Check these ranges if you are thinking of purchasing a player on the primary or secondary markets and begin to build a valuation for the player.

It is important that you do not solely rely on this data for forming your valuations as a number of factors also need to be taken into consideration:

- Rising/ falling Eth price – The selling ranges are only listed on Soraredata as Eth not in fiat so the variable rate of exchange with your local currency needs to be accounted for when making a decision on valuation; I always check the Sorare website as well to scan through recent sales figures in £ sterling as most other manager will base their sales on fiat not Eth.
- The increased popularity in Sorare – As interest gains in Sorare as will the demand for certain player cards which will in turn increase their cost, you cannot assume a players valuation will remain the same after 3 months if the user base has increased by 100,000 users.
- Changes in player's circumstances – Is the player injured and if so how long are they out? Has their leagues season come to an end? Have they just been promoted to the starting 11? Are they being heavily linked with a move to Abu Dhabi a league not covered by Opta? These are all factors you need to research before hitting the bid button.
- Official licensing of more teams to Sorare – As Sorare grows and acquires more teams it would be fair to assume that certain players prices will be affected e.g. more teams means more keepers which means less competition for the same few quality, regular keepers but this could well be negated by the fact there are so many more people playing Sorare!

You can begin to see the considerations we need to be making when deciding on which players we might want to buy and forming a price on those players.

Price history

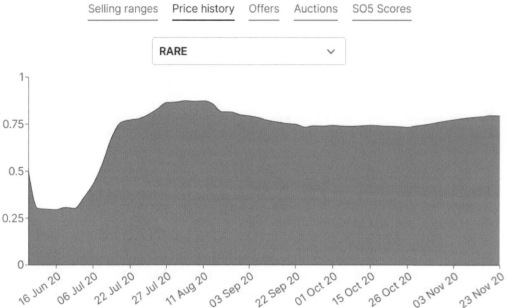

This is an at-a-glance look at the price history of a card, use the pick down list to select the scarcity of a card. We can see from this graph that Vlasic's Eth price jumped considerably at around the 6th July 2020 approximately 1 month before CSKA's 1st game of the 20/21 season; I would determine from this information that managers were buying Vlasic in preparation of the new Russian Premier League season.

Checking a player's price history could highlight to you a recent price drop due to injury or a significant rise due to links to a Champions League team.

Offers

This tab will let you know let you know if there are any current offers available on the player, click on the tab and you can select to see either Rare, Super Rare or Unique. Here we can see there is a Rare card for 6 Eth, the card has 24 hours 32 mins 29 seconds left on the market.

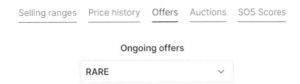

Ongoing offers

RARE ⌄

6.000 Ξ - 24:32:29

Auctions

Selling ranges   Price history   Offers   **Auctions**   SO5 Scores

Ongoing auctions

No auction available.

Ended auctions

Player	Card	Age	P	Price	Auction ended on	
Nikola Vlašić	9/10 (2020)	23	M	**3.146** Ξ	11/26/2020, 9:03:22 PM	Details
Nikola Vlašić	29/100 (2020)	23	M	**0.733** Ξ	11/22/2020, 11:15:04 AM	Details
Nikola Vlašić	27/100 (2020)	23	M	**0.918** Ξ	11/17/2020, 1:21:34 PM	Details
Nikola Vlašić	26/100 (2020)	23	M	**0.981** Ξ	11/11/2020, 8:15:00 PM	Details

From here you can see any ongoing or completed auctions along with the final price; if you click on 'Details' it will take you to that particular cards info and history including: Level Bonus and the bidding history.

S05 Scores

Gameweek	SO5 score
GW #119: 24-27 Nov 2020	63.20
GW #118: 20-24 Nov 2020	41.10
GW #114: 6-10 Nov 2020	74.70
GW #113: 3-6 Nov 2020	45.00
GW #112: 30 Oct-3 Nov 2020	59.50
GW #111: 27-30 Oct 2020	75.30
GW #110: 23-27 Oct 2020	100.00

This is the screen I use the most on Soraredata; the graph plots the players scores. The horizontal axis of the graph is the gameweek number and the vertical axis is scores from 0-100. Scores over 55 are coloured green, scores between 35-54 are yellow, scores below 34 are red and if they do not feature in the game it's noted as DNP (Did Not Play). Below the graph is a list of the latest gameweeks and their corresponding S05 score, if you click on the gameweek it will take you through to more details including starting lineups/ subs of both teams and how many minutes each player was on the pitch.

The graph is good for getting a quick impression of a player's output, we can see from Vlasic's scores that he is a consistently high scorer and that has been an attribute for many gameweeks.

However, do not simply dismiss a player if you see a run of red or yellow scores on the graph with the occasional green, sometimes it pays to dig a little deeper.

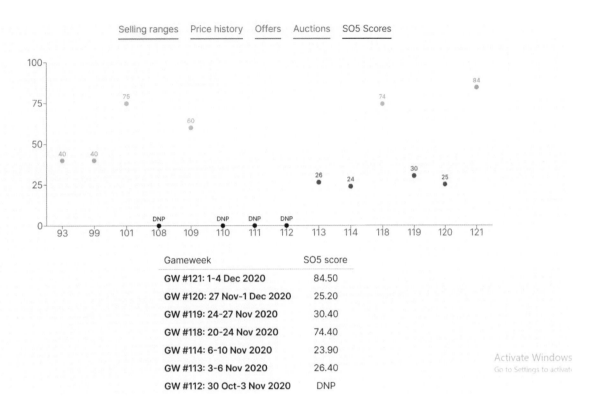

In the above SO5 Score profile, we can see this player has scored a high 84 in the last game but prior this there are quite a few reds or DNPS with the occasional good result going back 20 or so gameweeks. We might be wary of those reds and DNPS so need to do more investigating.

We can check on each of the gameweeks to get more detail:

- GW 121: Plays 90 mins – scores a goal and assists another – SO5 score 84.50
- GW 120: Plays 8 mins – SO5 score 25.20
- GW 119: Plays 77 mins – SO5 score 30.40
- GW 118: Plays 17 mins – scores a goal – SO5 score 74.40
- GW 114: Plays 3 mins – SO5 score 23.90
- GW 113: Plays 12 mins – SO5 score 26.40
- GW 112: DNP (Did Not Play)

Now we are starting to build a better picture, this player is getting increasing game time and when he gets the chance is making an impact on the game. Those red scores aren't reflecting a poor performance, just a lack of minutes.

The player is 21-year-old, AC Milan midfielder, Jen Hauge – not yet on Sorare at the time of writing but one to keep an eye on perhaps.

Hopefully at this point you've got a good idea about the fundamentals of the game and have been having a think about the sort of team you would like to put together so without further ado let's get started…

<u>7</u>
SIGNING UP & THE DRAFT

The sign-up process involves you becoming a 'Rookie Manager'; you are given the option to follow the Sorare onboarding process or having 400m (500m if you use this books referral link) to spend on your 10 Common cards. Once you have assembled your squad you are entered into the 8-week Rookie League; this is basically giving you a free taster of the Sorare game enabling you to familiarise yourself with how it is all structured and learn how to navigate around the website.

What process you follow will depend on how you plan to tackle Sorare from the off. Below I have listed the pros and cons of each method, which one you will choose will depend on if you want to gradually grow your squad with very little outlay or if you wish to start investing capital on cards early on:

Sorare Onboarding – If you choose this option you will be asked to take part in various tasks that teach you about Sorare, upon completing each of these tasks you will receive card packs as rewards, these cards will form your Rookie team.

Advantages – Can guarantee you some good quality starters in strong teams. Can allow you to have more expensive players than a manual draft. You will get 12 Common cards instead of 10.
Disadvantages – May receive players you do not want or not as many goalkeepers as you desire.

Recommended for: Those wanting to learn how Sorare works at a manageable pace and giving themselves the best chance to win rewards in the 8-week Rookie League.

Manual Draft Pick – This option will skip out the onboarding tutorial and go straight to the team selection page where you will manually pick your 10 Common card players ready to go straight into the gameweeks.

Advantages – Allows you to pick exactly what cards you want (budget allowing)/ have the option of picking 4 goalkeepers.
Disadvantages – Restricted by budget, unlikely you will be able to get as many good quality starters in your squad. Only get 10 Common cards as opposed to the 12 with the Onboarding.

Recommended for: Players who intend to start buying cards straight away, targeting S05 success early on and are not bothered about rewards in the Rookie League. If you are thinking about choosing this route I strongly suggest you do plenty of research prior to signing up.

If you aren't certain what route to go down, I suggest reading through this book in full to get a feel about how you want to approach Sorare. As with any investment it is always best to fully understand how it works before committing. When you have made your decision proceed to follow the guidance in the rest of this chapter.

Signing Up

Using the link below to sign up to Sorare will get you an additional 100 million to spend on Commons (so 500M instead of the standard 400M) plus once you have purchased 5 cards on the Primary market you will receive a free rare card, incredibly helpful and potentially worth a lot of money! [N.B The link will take you through to the Sorare home screen – there is no indication that you have the referral link, but it is embedded in the url so continue to follow the steps]

https://sorare.pxf.io/NnkbK

1) Hit the 'Sign Up' button in the top right-hand corner.

2) Complete the form that appears on your screen, your 'Nickname' will be your manager name that appears in the game – you can change this at a later date if required.

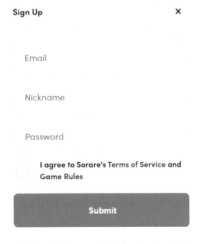

3) You will receive an email, go to your email account and click the button marked 'Confirm my account'.

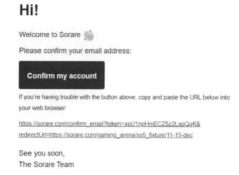

4) You will then be taken through to the first Sorare set up screen. DO NOT PRESS THE SKIP BUTTON. At this screen you can pick you club badge, nickname and club name. All these details can be changed later if you so wish. Complete the information and hit the 'Confirm' button.

5) The next screen will show your completed team information.

IMPORTANT:

- **IF YOU WISH TO CONTINUE WITH THE SORARE ONBOARDING – PRESS 'MEET MY SQUAD' (Continue to page 36)**

- **IF YOU WISH TO DO MANUAL DRAFTING PRESS SKIP IN THE TOP RIGHT HAND CORNER (Continue to Page 41)**

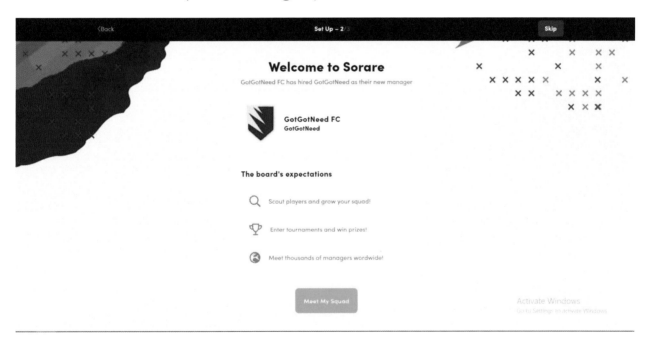

Sorare Onboarding Process

6) **This is important** You will be asked who your 3 favourite clubs are but it's important to note that the teams you select at this point will form the basis of your Rookie team. My recommendation here is to select 3 teams that fulfil the following criteria (listed below in order of priority):
   1) Have very good first choice goalkeepers (not long term injured and better if they are younger)
   2) Dominate their respective domestic league or are usually in contention to win the title
   3) Are involved in either the Champions/ Europa League, Asian Champions League or CONCACAF Champions League
   4) Ideally are currently active i.e. not out of season or on a winter break

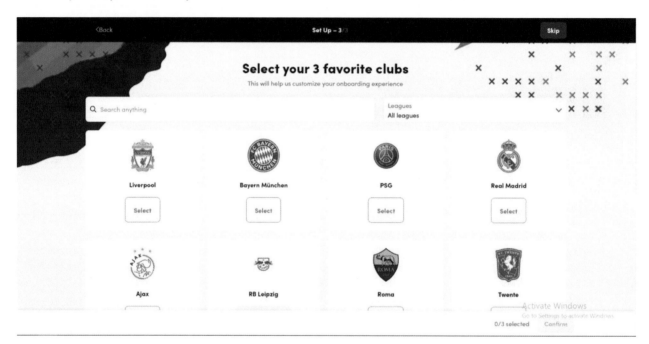

You are able to select from the variety of available leagues by clicking the drop-down bar in the top right-hand corner. I would recommend that, if possible, you try and select 2 teams from Europe and 1 team from either the MLS or the Asian Leagues, this will give you a chance to have a viable goalkeeper option in the SO5s all year round i.e. your Asian keeper will step in when the European Leagues come to the end of their season and vice-versa.

The reason we are choosing teams based on these criteria is:

a) Goalkeepers are the most expensive cards on Sorare due to their increased scarcity compared to other positions – a football squad will generally have 3 goalkeepers but only 1 of them will be the regular starter, compare that to defenders or midfielders who you may have a selection of 6 you can start to see why those keepers will be a commodity; for this reason many see purchasing a starting goalkeeper as a barrier to entry on Sorare however good quality Common goalkeepers can be used in the full SO5 D4 tournaments, although subject to a -45% deduction to any points they gain in a gameweek, they can still enable you to finish within the rewards if your goalkeeper has a good scoring gameweek.

b) Selecting good quality teams will give us the best chance of getting high scoring Common card outfield players to utilise in the Rookie League.

Remember, the cards we get going forward are luck of the draw but using the above team selection criteria you are giving yourself the best opportunity to receive those premium cards.

For further guidance on how to pick your teams see 'Resources for picking teams or players' on page 45.

Once you have made your 3 team selections hit the 'Confirm' button in the bottom right-hand corner.

7) You will now see the screen overleaf and will start receiving your first card pack. From this point on follow all the steps and upon completion of the tasks you will be rewarded with more cards until you have all 12 Common cards, this is actually a nice process to go through to familiarise yourself with the Sorare website. Fingers crossed you get some good ones!

8) The final task is to make a bid on a player, if like me, you will not be ready at this stage to start buying players but there is a simple way to complete this task without spending any money. Proceed to follow the task steps.

9) When you are at the stage where you need to make a bid, search for the best player you can think of that is currently up for auction, you want to find a premium player that is quite new on the auctions and has a very low price (so just a few £, $, €), below I have found Oblak at €8.07.

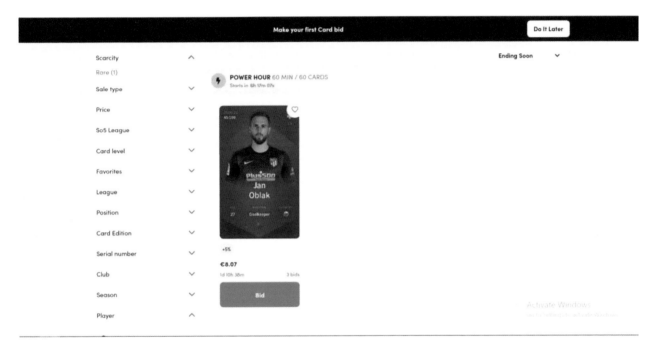

10) Press the blue button marked 'Bid' and you will open the bidding window, make sure the option is on 'Credit Card', add your card details and make a minimal bid. The task will now be completed but the likelihood is that you will be outbid and the money not removed from your card. In the extreme off-chance that your bid is the winning one you will of got a very good player for a really low cost.

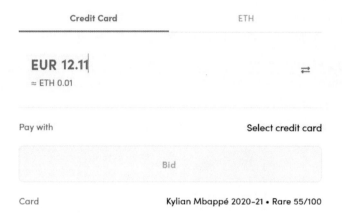

The Onboarding process is now complete, and you will have received your 12 Common Cards ready for your first gameweek.

Manual Draft Pick

1) Once you have picked to skip the Sorare Onboarding Process you will be taken to the screen below. To begin your draft picks click on the blue bar at the top that says 'Claim my first 10 free cards'.

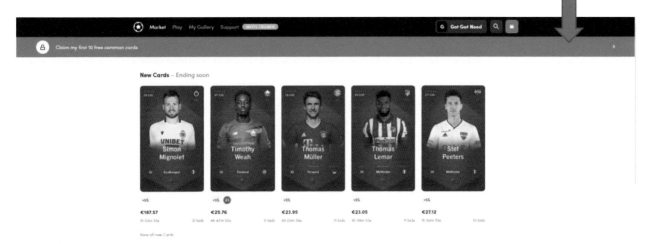

2) The draft pick screens will appear, read the dialogue boxes and hit the blue button marked 'Next' on Steps 1 and 2

Compose a 5-a-side football team

You can select players from the top 20 leagues to build the most competitive 5-a-side team. With fantasy football, the most important criteria is making sure your player is a starter on his team.

Next

3) **<u>This is important</u>** – When you get to Step 3 asking what type of manager you are make sure you select 'Advanced – Build Your Own Team' as this will allow you to pick the players you want to fit your preferred route.

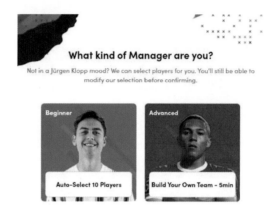

4) You are now at the stage where you can begin picking your squad; you have £500m to spend (if you used the link), each player has a price below their name, as you pick players their price is deducted from your bank balance. Players prices are correlated with their auction market price so you will see the best players are usually the most expensive!

In order to get involved in SO5 tournaments you are going to need to start buying cards either at auction or the secondary market, we will look at how to do this in the next chapter.

Planning ahead then, you will want to use this Manual Draft to your advantage, setting yourself up for your time in the SO5s and training up players, there is one major way to do this – Goalkeepers – lots of them!

Goalkeepers are expensive on Sorare, of all the cards on the platform they are in shortest supply and then when you consider that Goalkeepers are very rarely rotated the ones that play regulary are in high demand.

My suggestion is that you use the Rookie draft to acquire 4 first choice goalkeepers and preferably score highly; use the method of scouting on Sorare Data discussed in the previous chapter to find goalkeepers with high scoring and starting averages. If you can get a goalkeeper from each of the 4 SO5 tournaments (Champions Europe, Challenger Europe, Champions Asia, Champions America) even better but this may be a big ask with your bank balance.

For the other 6 positions in your team you will want to fill them with the cheapest players as possible (10m each) so that your bank can be spent on the goalkeepers. If these can be good players too even better [refer to 'The Real Betis Cheatcode' on page 49]

Picking goalkeepers gives you two options within the SO5 tournaments:

A) Common goalkeepers can be used in D4 tournaments, although they are subject to a -45% deduction to any points they gain in a gameweek this can still enable you to finish within the cards if your goalkeeper has a good score

B) The more goalkeepers you have the more training teams you can enter, these are really useful when you have a lot of players who cant get into SO5 tournaments for one reason or another but you stil want them to earn XP

Having a regular starting common goalkeepers from each of the SO5 leagues can give you the option to enter those leagues should you acquire the outfield players to do so.

5) Picking your team once you have a strategy is pretty straightforward, just select the player you want and they will filled into your squad and their price will be deducted from your bank.

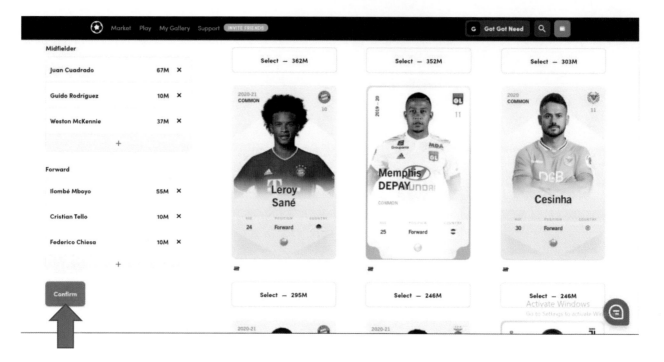

For further guidance on how to pick your teams see 'Resources for picking teams or players' on page 45.

Once you are happy with your team press 'Confirm'.

You are now all complete and will be taken through to the Sorare homescreen ready to enter the next Rookie League gameweek.

Resources for picking teams or players

There are a few points of reference that can help in assisting to pick your 3 teams or if your players if you pick the manual draft:

Sorare Data:
Access the website and click on the header listed 'Rankings' then 'Player Rankings'

You will bring up the screen below, from here you can filter players by the SO5 league they play in, their position (I have selected Goalkeepers) and whether they qualify for the Under 23 leagues.
The players will be listed in ranking order of their average score from the last 15 games (L15 AVG), if you click on any of the headers it will relist the players in order of that particular ranking. The columns listed as '% GMS L5' and '% GMS L15' tell you how many games of the last 5 and 15 games that player has started. You can also see the average 1-month auction sale prices of the players in the respective scarcities.

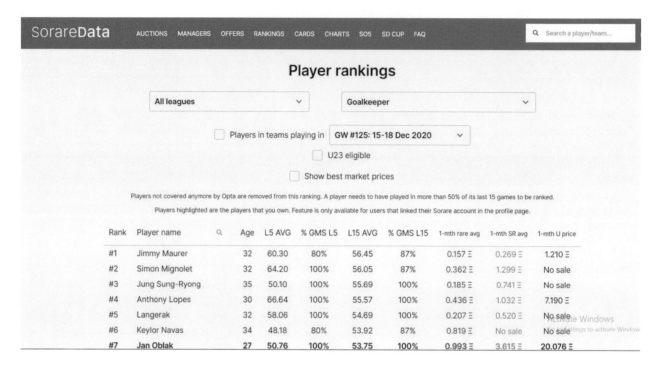

We can see that Jimmy Maurer is the top performing keeper in the last 15 games, however it is also worth noting that he has started 80% of the last 5 games – potentially he could be injured or being rotated, this would need further investigating. As previously mentioned, I would suggest that you aim for goalkeeper with a very high starting average for your Rookie team to ensure they give you the best utility.

Try scrolling through the list of players and checking if there are any stand outs in terms of high average scores and level of starting games, if they play for big teams in their respective leagues make a note of them for your shortlist.

Injury/ Transfer/ Team News

There are several helpful websites and apps which can help inform you on the latest team news. Before you shortlist a team based upon their starting goalkeeper check to see they are free from injury, you don't want to target a player only to find out they are out for the rest of the season. Also, research to see if a long-term injury is potentially ruling them out or if they have any transfer speculation that could see them moved out of the Sorare/ Opta covered leagues.

My personal go-to sites are: -

- Twitter.com – I find this to be the quickest way to get the latest player and team news, there are various fan profiles, scouts and official clubs feeds that give up-to-the minute information on injuries, transfers and any speculation. I often direct message trusted people to ask their opinion on players or for background information – this is particularly helpful when you are researching smaller leagues such as Belgium or Japan.
- Sportsgambler.com/football/injuries-suspensions – This is a very useful site that lists every injured or suspended player in most major leagues.
- Transfermarkt.com – This site has everything including latest transfer rumours and injuries, search a player and it will bring up their bio and if injured it will state how long they are out for.
- Fotmob.com – A good reference site and also an app, you can save your favourite players for quick reference and it will tell you if they are injured or suspended and how long they are expected to be out.

Always double check the information you are provided with other resources, sometimes the above sites are slow being updated or their own sources of information are incorrect.

Fixture lists

Depending on when you sign up to Sorare and do your draft you will need to be aware of the various differing footballing calendars so that you don't pick any players that have a season coming to a finish or break, for example if you are doing your draft in December you should be aware that the Russian League usually has a winter break from the last week of December to the end of February so no point in filling your draft with RPL players.

As an approximate guide:

European Leagues run August/ September to May (Russia has winter break December-March)
Asian Leagues run to February/ March to December
North American Leagues (MLS) run March/April to December
South American Leagues run year round (better to check these carefully as they can be a mindfield)

Before you pick a player makes sure they have a busy fixture list with either league games or Champions/ Europa League games for the duration of your Rookie League avoiding any players that have a short break or a run of domestic cup games as these will not earn you points in gameweeks.

The sites and apps below are good for checking fixtures lists: -

- Whoscored.com
- Sofascore.com

Discord

The Sorare developers and community is very active on Discord, there is an abundance of information available to all members and the official announcments are usually put out here first. If there is something particular you want to find out with any aspect of the game you can always post the question on the relevant thread and more often than not someone will reply quickly with a helpful answer or point you in the right direction.

Make sure to set up a Discord account when you join Sorare and join the official group using this link:

https://discord.gg/tDzgG74

The Real Betis Cheat Code

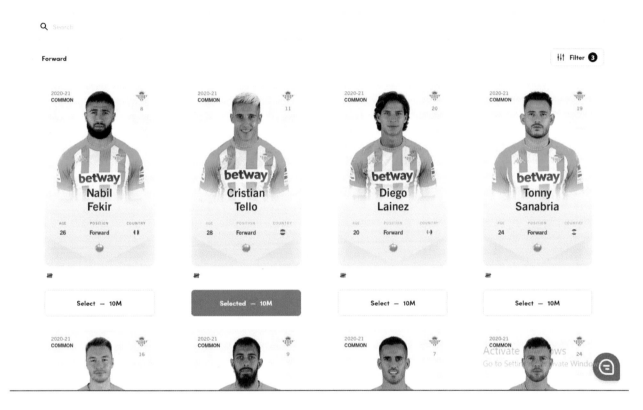

It took me a while to actually find out what was going on with this quirk whilst doing my rookie draft but I'm I stumbled upon it as it freed up a lot of money and the background story is great.

Whilst picking your draft players use the filters to bring up Real Betis players only, you will notice that every one of their players is only 10m even their most regular, high performing stars so effectively you could fill a whole rookie squad of 10 players for just 100m leaving you 400m spare in the bank which gives you plenty of options to spend on quality, high scoring players from other teams.

The reason Real Betis players are only 10m is down to their fierce rivalry with their city neighbours, Sevilla whose home kit is red. The rivalry runs so deep that Real Betis refuse to be associated with the colour red in any way and when signing up to their Sorare partnership they had it written into the contract that no Real Betis player would be pictured on a card with a red background ruling out any Rare cards.

Common cards are allocated their prices by drawing from their recent auction sales of equivalent Rare cards and as Real Betis do not have any Rare cards they default to the cheapest cost of 10m.

Depending on your chosen strategy route I would defintely suggest picking the Real Betis first choice goalkeeper and then checking SorareData to see who their highest scoring, regular performers are then selecting at least one defender, midfielder and forward from their team coming to a total of 50m; this leaves you a good bank to select either a team that can be competitive in the Rookie league or allow you to pick up three other 1st choice goalkeepers.

<u>8</u>
GAMEWEEK

Gameweeks occur twice a week 1) Fridays 17.00 ending Tuesday at 05.00 and 2) Tuesdays 17.00 ending Fridays at 05.00.

You need to make sure your teams are selected and confirmed before the 5pm deadline otherwise they will not be entered.

To go to to the team selection page click play and then the forthcoming gameweek which will say 'OPEN' in green.

The next screen you see will be the gameweek page where you can begin making your team selection:

1) This informs you what gameweek number you have open, how long until the deadline closes (yellow text) and if you have any teams selected.
2) The gameweek period (dates and times)
3) From here you can select from the 'Main' screen which shows you SO5 league information or 'Matches' which will show you which games are being played in that gameweek which are represented within the SO5 leagues

Scroll further down the screen and you will be able to see all the SO5 tournaments open for that gameweek:

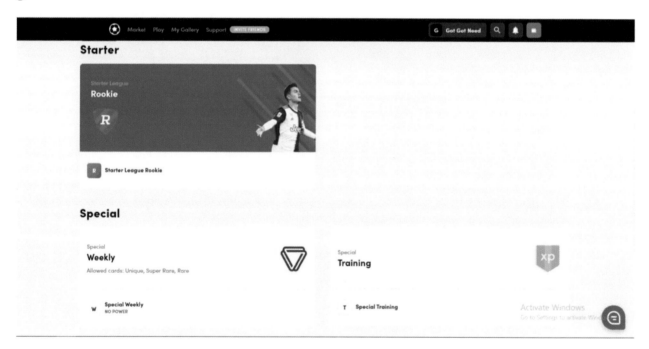

Here we can see that the Rookie League, Special Weekly and Training League are all available for selection. Below the header for the League you will be able to see what cards qualify for it and if there are any other criteria e.g. in the Special Weekly Unique, Super Rare and Rare cards are all allowed and no power will be applied to cards.

Click on 'Starter Rookie League to be taken through to the team builder screen:

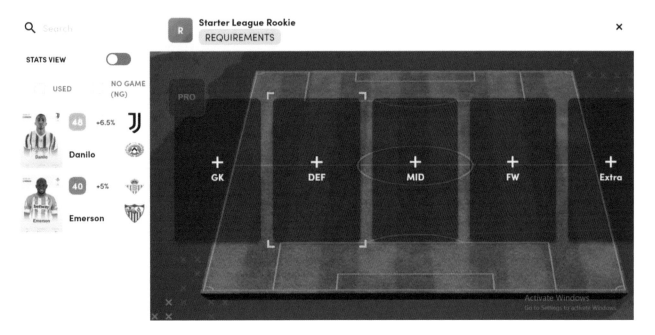

If you hover over the grey bar marked 'REQUIREMENTS' it will show you the card criteria for the selected league, we can see that a max of 2 Rares can be used in the Starter League Rookie all other must be Commons.

As you select each position it will bring up your card options, we are currently on Defender and can see our 2 defender cards, Danilo and Emerson.

Within the players details are:

- Average score for the last 5 games (Danilo has 48, Emerson has 40,)
- The card's bonus (Danilo has +6.5%, Emerson has +5%)
- Opposition in this gameweek (Danilo has Udinese, Emerson has Sevilla)

By clicking on the 'PRO' tab you can see the player's scores for the last 5 games.

For this gameweek it looks like Danilo would be our best choice due to current form but you will need to think about a number of factors when choosing your strongest team [See 'Tips For Team Selection' on page 56].

Once you have selected your player they will fill the spot in your team, repeat this step until you have your whole team in place.

The 5ᵗʰ Spot

The 'Extra' or 5ᵗʰ spot in your team can be allocated to any outfield postion, its up to you who you think may be strongest in a particular gameweek to score highest but to date average historic scoring shows that statistically midfielders and defenders score highest most often. Use your 5ᵗʰ spot wisely as it can make or break a successful gameweek.

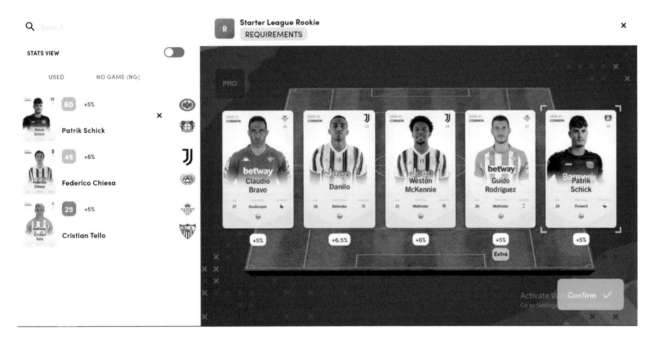

Once you are happy with your team selection you can press the green button at the bottom right marked 'Confirm' and your team will be saved ready for the start of the gameweek.

You can change your selections at any time before the deadline closes, it is worth monitoring the news right up until the last minute in case an injury to one of your teams is announced or a manager may give a strong indication that one of your players won't be in the starting 11.

Choosing Captain

Gameweek selection in the SO5s is slightly different to the Rookie League as you will need to choose a Captain for each of your teams, the captain will earn an additional +20% of level bonus to their score so choosing the right player can be the difference in making the rewards. Your captain should be your best player that gameweek and usually the first on the teamsheet. As mentioned previously, defenders and midfielders on average score higher more often but you may feel confident your forward will bag a couple of goals in which case they could be a good shout. Time to make the big calls!

Tips For Team Selection

Below is a breakdown of considerations I take and resources that I personally use when picking between players on a any particular gameweek, this is by no means exhaustive and as you get into the game you will pick up your own system of working to filter your strongest team:

1. **Player form** – Stating the obvious but we want our player to score as highly as possible and if a player is in a good run of form that can make our decision a lot easier, likewise if we have a player that has been performing terribly recently we may want to steer clear. The average score on the Sorare team builder screen can a good initial indicator but it doesn't give a full story and I like to go to SorareData to check the scores for the last 15, how many games they have been starting and generally how many minutes per game they play

2. **Team form** – Our player is more likely to score higher if his team is dominating the opposition; I will check whoscored.com who provide a useful match preview feature which shows the likely lineups, the team's form and head-to-head data from when the teams have previously met, you will also be able to check the team's standing in the league.

3. **Team/ player news** – I will always check to see if there is major team or player news which could affect performace or making the starting 11. I use the apps FotMob and Sofascore to check each of my player selections to see if they are currently suspended or ruled out with injury (you can save your favourite players/ teams on both apps to bring them up quicker). I will also search player names and clubs on Twitter to see if there is any breaking news regarding team selections or injuries.

4. **SorareData** – Our trusty friends at SorareData have a really useful feature for identifying your best lineup in the SO5 tournaments, on the drop down menu under your name select 'Your players breakdown'.

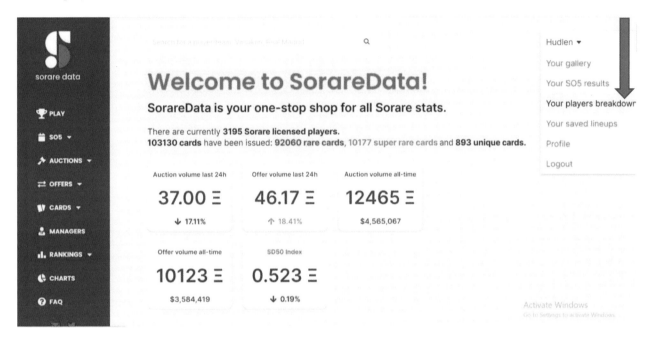

This will bring up the team builder screen (opposite), from here you can set a number of criteria to help identify your best possible lineup: choose the gameweek you are setting up and the Division you are targetting, you can then select the position you picking, whether they are a starter/ sub or reserve and if they have any known injury or suspension.

In the following example we are choosing a keeper who is a starter and has no known injuries or suspensions:

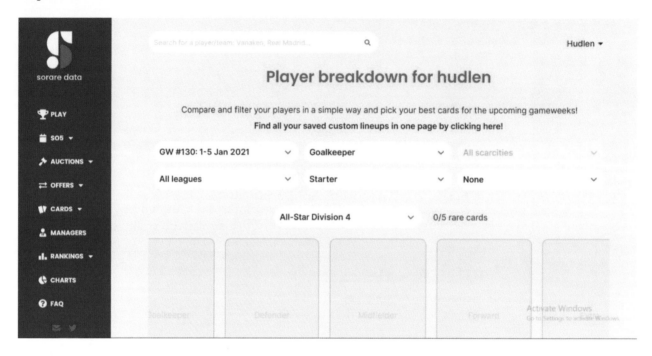

Once you have set your conditions you can scroll down the page and see the players that are available to you that fulfill the criteria (below). We can see that our options are either Valencia's Jaume Doménech or Atletico's Jan Oblak:

Got Got Need by Daniel Higgs

Eligible players

Opp avg = average score of starting players of this position that played (over the last 10 games) against the player next opponent. Player injury status is subject to last minute changes and should not be considered as a reliable source. **Always do your own research.**

☑ Show already picked players ☑ Power adjusted scores

Player name	Card	Bonus	L5	L15	Last 15 scores (new to old)	Gameweek opponent	Opp G avg	Status
Jaume Doménech Starter - 30	36/100 (2019)	2.5%	62 80%	54 93%	NP 86 44 70 48 35 68 48 / 36 49 65 69 48 47 46	Cádiz CF Home	46	✓
Jan Oblak Starter - 27	12/100 (2020)	8.0%	56 100%	55 100%	69 50 28 65 68 37 77 65 / 70 75 36 46 38 80 21	Deportivo Alavés Away	42	✓

We can see the details for each player including the bonus level, their average score for last 5 and 15 games, their next opponent and one of SorareData's neatest data sets – the average score of the player position who played the opposition in the last 10 games. So we can see that Doménech is playing Cadiz at home, the average score of a goalkeeper who played Cadiz is 46 whereas Oblak is away to Deportivo where the average goalkeeper scores 42. Doménech also has a higher average score in last 5 games so he would appear to be the strongest choice in this instance but it would also depend on the other previous considerations we have taken into account.

Targeting S05 Tournaments

Depending on the cards you have at your disposal you will need to make choices on which S05 tournaments to enter, this particularly becomes true when your gallery begins to grow.

There are several schools of thought about the best approach but ultimately it comes down to your preference. The Global SO5 has the added prize benefit of Eth for hitting certain threshold scores which is great for putting money back in the pot but the Global is by far the most popular tournament and one of the hardest to win whilst the cards you claim as rewards can be from any league and age bracket which can make gallery building less of a certainty.

59

My personal method is to target the SO5 tournaments where I would like to gains cards e.g. if I am looking to collect more U23 player cards I will put the strongest possible line-up in the Global U23 Division 4, if I then have a surplus of U23 cards I will then build a line-up in the Global or even the Global U23 D3 if I feel they have a chance of winning something. In my mind I have a prioritised list of tournaments I want to enter, and I will fill line-ups in that order.

Some weeks you will have to adapt your gameplan as certain players won't have matches and you will need to reassess which SO5 you feel you can field a strong lineup.

Training

Once you have completed your SO5 teams you may be left with a surplus of players who you cannot fit into your teams or are not playing in that gameweek for one reason or another, these players should be put into training so that they still accumulate some XP.

Training teams are picked in the same way as a standard SO5, you will need a goalkeeper, defender, midfielder, forward and an extra outfield player. Common goalkeepers really come in handy here as having that surplus enables you to fill as many training teams as possible and get your players earning so that when they do enter the SO5 they have that extra bonus.

Players in training will accumulate 75 XP points but the XP is enhanced if they are actually playing or in the same training team as players who are active in a game.

Watching the results

Once the gameweek kicks off and your teams lock in you will be able to view their progress in the gameweek screen. Click on the tab marked 'Play' and then select the 'Live' gameweek.

From this page you can navigate around to find out how your players have scored or currently doing in live matches. When you get to the business end of the gameweek it can get really exciting if you need a certain number of points from one of your players to achieve a podium place. If you click this drop-down box you can toggle between confirmed, live or pending player's scores.

Below we are viewing our confirmed player's scores, we can see that Patrik Schick scored 40 and Guido Rodriguez scored 52.

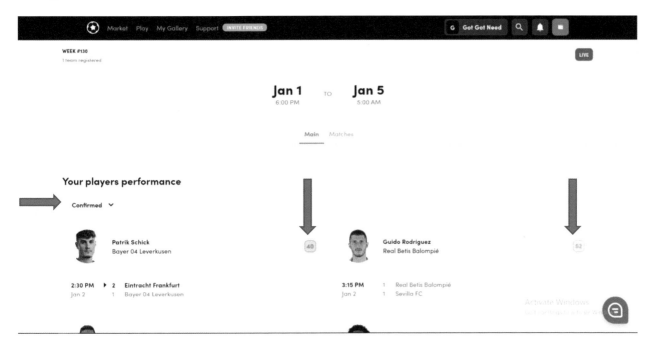

If you click on one of your players you will bring up a breakdown of their score:

Scroll further down and you will be able to see where you currently stand in any tournaments you have entered. This will update throughout the gameweek as your players complete matches and opposing manager's teams also perform. You won't know your exact final position until all the gameweek matches are complete. SorareData also have a useful gameweek feature that presents your progress along with calculations for potential finishing position and any rewards you may be in line for.

At the bottom of the page, you will see the 3 highest scoring players from each position in the gameweek and below that is the prize pool details tab.

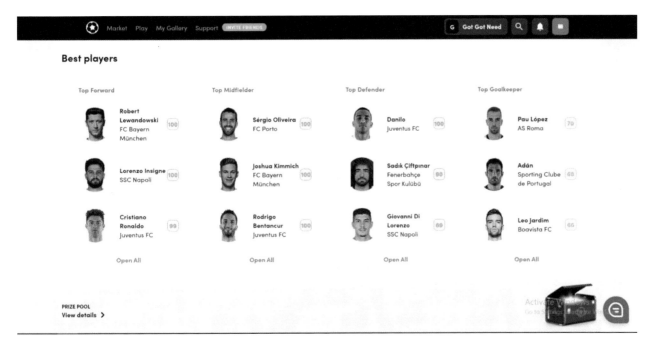

Clicking on the prize pool tab will bring up the prize breakdown for any tournaments you have entered.

Card prizes are categorised by tiers, Tier 1 being the best. Cards are allocated tiers based upon their recent sale prices at auction. The card prize you receive will always be from the tournament entered i.e. if you win a Tier 2 card in the Champion Europe SO5 you will receive a Tier 2 Champion Europe player.

We can see by bringing up the Prize pool details for the Rookie Starter League that there ae 2619 participants (top right), 1st place gets a Tier 1 Rare, 2nd and 3rd get a Tier 2 Rare, 4th and the top 10% get a Star common, the remaining top 50% get a Tier 1 common. By clicking on Tier details at the bottom you can view what cards fall into which Tier.

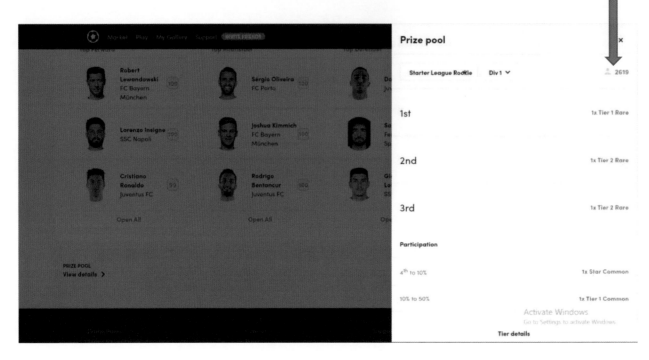

The chances of getting a top 3 place are really stacked against you but it's quite achievable to get top 10% which could easily mean you get another very good Common goalkeeper to take into the full SO5 tournaments/ training.

SorareData has a great feature for tracking your SO5 result too, click under your name 'Your SO5 results' and you will bring up the screen opposite which shows you your current tournament position in the gameweek (79th) and your current points score (292.83)

If you scroll further down you will see a breakdown of your player's scores with any bonuses applied. It will also tell you where you place percentage wise in all the particpants (top 3.02%), it will also indicate where you could possibly finish calculated from the teams below you in the tournament, so we can see we are currently 79th but could finish 90th if all the teams below us score enough points, obviously this can make for some nervous watching once all your players have completed their games.

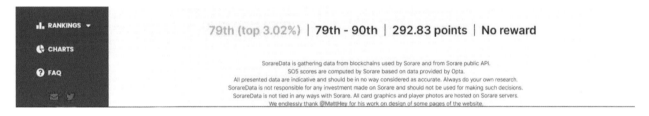

At the end of the gameweek and once all the Opta scores are finalised you will be notified by email and within the game of your final positions within any SO5 tournaments you have entered, if you are lucky/skilled enough to end up in the rewards then you will also be able to find out what you've won – exciting times!

Got Got Need by Daniel Higgs

9
BUYING ETH

It's more than likely that once you have familiarised yourself with how Sorare works and you've participated in a few Rookie tournaments you'll start eyeing up the markets for your first purchase.

In order to buy cards at the markets you can either use a debit/ credit card which incurs a 10% surcharge or have Eth loaded up in your Sorare account (or wallet as its often referred to). Whilst the card payment option may seem convenient you need to account for that 10% fee when bidding and be cautious as your card provider may occasionally temporarily suspend your bank account if they see lots of activity on your account from bids.

Sorare are continually making improvements additions to the payment options; below I have listed the main 2.

Option 1 – Ramp

The simplest method at the time of writing is to use Ramp who are an external Fiat to Crypto payments provider that Sorare have partnered with, you can read more about them here: https://ramp.network/

I have used the Ramp funding option myself and found it easy and straightforward enough – they did carry out some additional identity verification checks on me before they would release my Eth, but I found it assuring that they practiced this due diligence and all the advisors I dealt with were polite and prompt in their responses.

To use Ramp follow the steps below:

1) Click on the blue button at the top right of the screen (it has a wallet image)

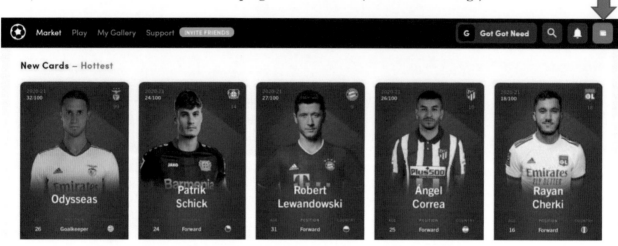

1) Click on the option that says 'Fund With Ramp'

2) You will link with the Ramp Network and will see the form below. The form tells you what the current exchange rate is. Add how much Fiat (£, $, €) you would like to convert, the form will tell you how much Eth you will receive in return along with the calculated fees – if you are ok press the blue button marked 'Proceed'.

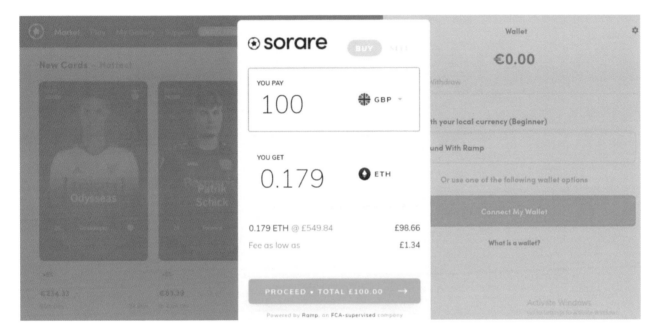

3) You will be asked to enter your email address and agree to the terms and conditions. Once you have completed this step you will receive a verification email, follow the steps entering your payment details, the Eth should appear in your Sorare account within a few minutes depending on how busy the blockchain is.

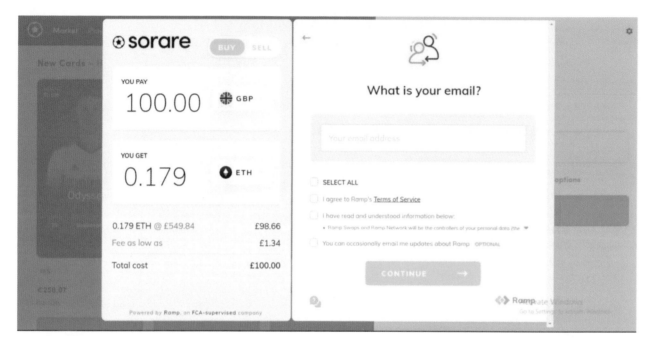

Using the Ramp method is quick, easy and accessible for all but there is a commission fee payable and you won't get the best exchange rate.

Option 2 – Fund via Coinbase

If you want to secure the best rate of exchange and also pay as little commission fees then this is the option you will want to use. Coinbase is a reputable crypto exchange platform, they also have a Crypto trading platform called Coinbase Pro which although more technical has much smaller fees and will allow you to set your desired price for buying Eth.

1) First thing you need to do is setup a Coinbase account, if you use this referral link you will receive £7.32 worth of Bitcoin once you have spent £73.30 on Eth for Sorare:
https://www.coinbase.com/join/higgs_ww
Follow the steps to complete the sign-up process.

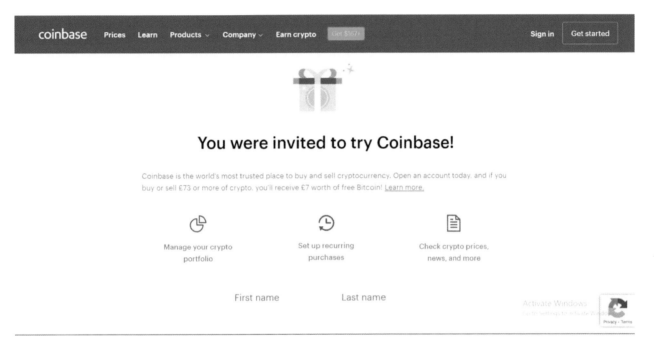

1) Once you have your Coinbase account setup you will now be able to use the Coinbase Pro trading platform via this website: **https://pro.coinbase.com/trade/ETH-GBP** use the exact same login details for Coinbase if you are prompted. You will bring up the trading interface:

2) There is a lot of stuff going on in this screen but once you get used to the information in front of you navigating around will become second nature. You will need to load some money into your Coinbase account and then the aim is to purchase Eth at the best possible rate. I recommend following this walkthrough in order to do this: **https://blockonomi.com/coinbase-pro-review**

3) Once you have purchased your Eth you will then need to create a holding wallet to send your crypto to, there are a few options for this but Metamask is established, secure and reliable. Access the website **https://metamask.io/** and follow the download steps.

4) Your Metamask wallet will have a unique address (a long series of numbers and letters) also referred to as a Public Key; in order to send Eth to your wallet you will need to use this address. It can be found at the top of your Metamask homepage, it will automatically be copied when you click on it so it can be pasted quickly when doing transactions.

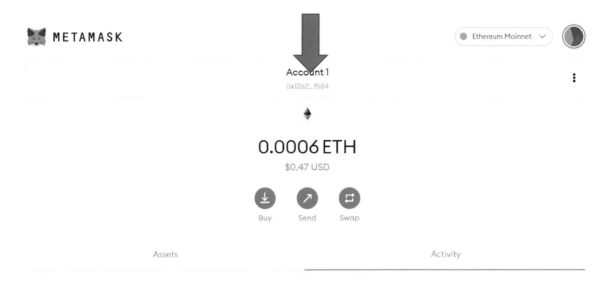

5) Move the Eth you purchased on Coinbase into your Metamask wallet, if you are feeling unsure or want to practice doing this try sending a small denomination to help familiarise yourself with the process. The amount of time the transaction takes to complete can vary depending on the blockchain, I have had it happen instantaneously sometimes but have also waited for quite a few hours.

6) You will now need to connect your Metamask wallet to your Sorare account, this is a straightforward process. Go to Sorare and click on the wallet icon, click the option that says, 'Connect to Wallet', this will bring up a Metamask pop-up screen and you just need to complete your log-in details. This should complete the connection between your Metamask and Sorare, you will now see your Eth in your Sorare account.

Once you've got your wallets linked and you have money in your Sorare account you will be ready to hit the markets.

Got Got Need by Daniel Higgs

10
BUYING, SELLING & TRADING

Acquiring players and building a gallery to suit your own personal style is a really exciting aspect of Sorare.

There are 3 ways to obtain player cards other than as rewards: -

- Buying at auction (New Signings)
- Buying from other managers (Transfer Market)
- Buying from other managers (Direct Offers)

Each method requires its own approach, and it can be easy to pay over the odds if you have not done your research.

Before you get started my first recommendation is to search every player you have an interest in and save them to your favourites by following them, this will allow you to easily filter players of interest when trawling the various marketplaces and you will also receive an email alert when a new card is released into the auctions. You are also able to follow players who aren't yet on the Sorare platform which can be really helpful when a new team is released notifying you that one of your favourite players will soon be on the market.

To search a player, click on the magnify glass icon in the top tool bar, this will bring up a search bar enter the desired player's name and if they are registered on the platform (within a licensed team or not) they will come up for selection.

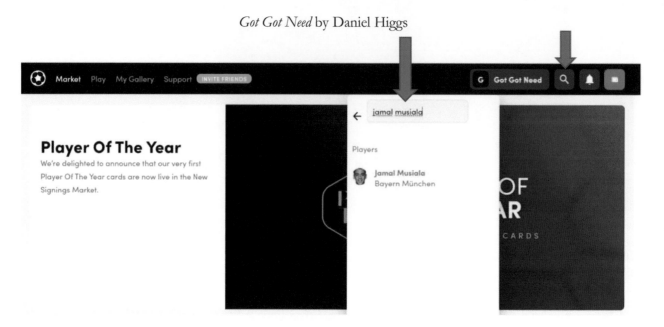

Click on the player's name and it will take you through to their profile page, click on the button marked 'Follow' and the button will change to say 'Following', they will now be saved to your favourites. You can also save teams to your favourites list doing this process.

Buying at Auction

The New Signings/ Auctions are, for me, the most exciting way to buy new players. Sorare release new season cards into the market, this happens randomly, sometimes 2 cards can come on within hours of each other, sometimes you can wait weeks just to see one.

The auctions are constantly running and there will be times when a card you are after finishes in the early hours of morning – if you are prepared to set an alarm you can sometimes pick up a bargain!

There are also the Power Hours where 60 cards are released into the marketplace for a flash 60-minute auction. Power Hours generally happen at the following times:

- Monday 21.00-22.00 UTC
- Tuesdays 15.00-16.00
- Wednesdays 07.00-08.00 UTC
- Thursdays 21.00-22.00 UTC
- Fridays 15.00-16.00 UTC
- Saturdays 07.00-08.00 UTC
- Sundays 21.00-22.00 UTC

The Power Hours on Sundays are usually when the premium players/ cards are released and can be a big event within the community.

Cards start at a set € price depending on their scarcity:

- Rares @ €5
- Super Rares @ €50
- Uniques @ €500

There are also Bundle auctions where 5 cards are lumped together in one package, these can be players from the same team or league. They can sometimes offer good value and you could pick up a whole ready-made team, but you need to assess what players are making up the bundle before committing. To access the Auctions hover over the 'Market' header on the homescreen and select 'New Signings'

You will now be on the New Signings page, the cards ending soonest are displayed unless you change the option in the right-hand drop-down menu to the other alternatives of newly listed, highest price or lowest price. On the left-hand side are the filter options, scroll down the filters and you will see 'Favourites', this will usually be the first filter I apply so that I am only viewing players I have shortlisted.

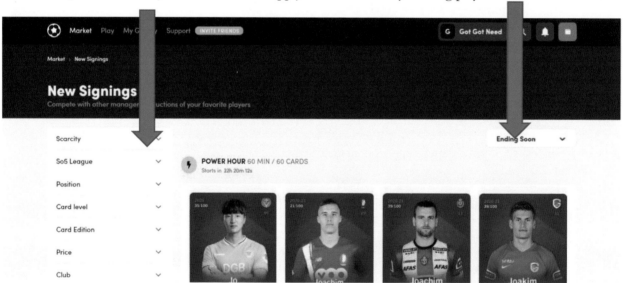

I have now applied my filter of 'Favourites' bringing up all the player cards that match that criteria. On each card you will be able to see the auction time remaining, the current highest bid and the card's level bonus (this will always be +5% on the new signings market), the '23' denotes that the player is 23 years old or under. Below the players card is the blue 'Bid' button which you can press if you want to bid on a card.

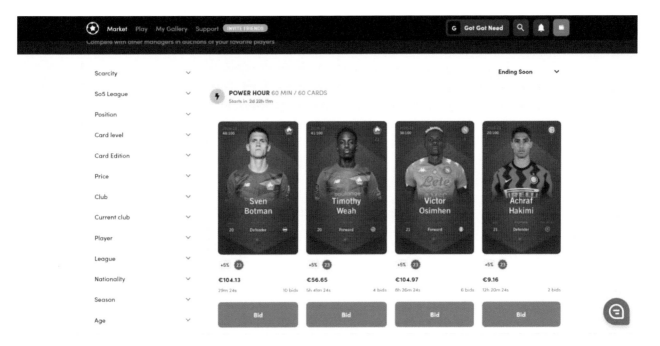

If you click on a card it will bring up the bidding history to date including the bid denominations and who is bidding, you are able to click on bidders names and view their galleries something that can be handy if you want to judge the competion!

If you choose to make a bid press either of the blue 'Bid' buttons and a pop up will appear providing you your payment options (credit card or Eth), the bidding will automatically go up by a minimum 10% increment however you can enter your own price if you feel this will deter other bidders or you have a maximum figure in mind that you want to go straight in with.

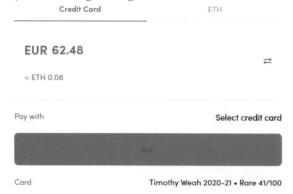

If you are bidding with Credit/ Debit card please be aware that each bid will be reported to your card provider although only a winning bid will actually go through as a transaction, this high level of activity can sometimes cause your card to be temporarily suspended by your provider – definitely worth keeping in mind if there is an auction you are targeting.

If you win an auction the player will show as 'Transfer in Progress' and the card will be moved to your gallery once the transaction is all confirmed on the blockchain. Well done, you are now the owner of that card forever!

The Transfer Market – Buying and Selling

All managers can list their own cards on the Transfer Market (except Common cards). When cards are listed, they go on the market for 48 hours.

The manager chooses what a card is listed for and if another manager likes that price they can buy the card there and then. At the time of writing there is no commission charged by Sorare for transactions between managers.

To access the Transfer Market hover over the 'Market' header on the home screen and select 'Transfer Market'

On the Transfer Market landing page you will see all the players listed by other managers, on the screen below I have already applied the 'Favourites' filter and sorted the cards by Lowest Price first. We can see that the cheapest Timothy Weah is €120.55/ 0.120 Eth being sold by the manager Richmond T, if you are happy with that price you can click the 'Buy Now' button, or you can click the card itself to open up further details.

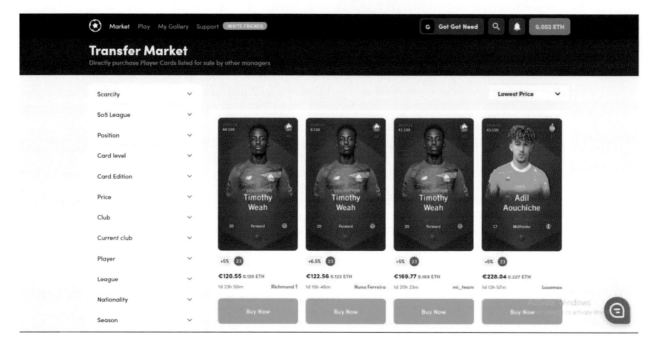

We have clicked into the card itself and can see more of this individual card's details including the players last five SO5 scores. You will notice that you can click on the selling managers name to go through to their profile.

Scroll further down the page to see the cards history, this tells us who has owned the card previously, how much they were purchased for and when transactions took place. This card was originally won as a reward by DJKoeft, it was then transferred twice between 2 managers as direct offers which are always undisclosed fees, finally it was bought by the current manager for €99.45/ 0.099 Eth on 7th January 2020. If you click on the Players name at the bottom of the page you will bring up every card that player has on Sorare including any that are currently on sale either at auction or transfer market and all the sold card prices with dates – a useful exercise to do cost comparisons.

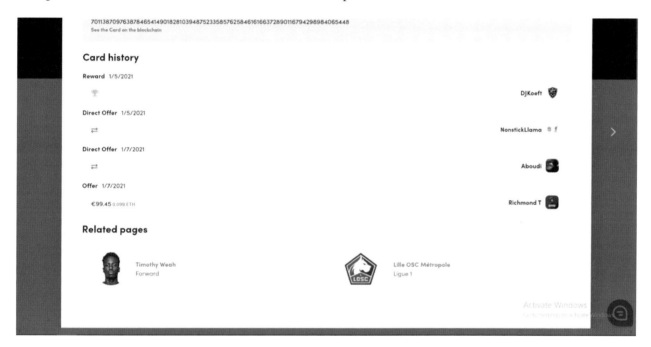

Clicking into the Manager'profile page I am now able to view their gallery of cards, I can see their club name, their Discord profile, how long they have been on Sorare and how many cards they own.

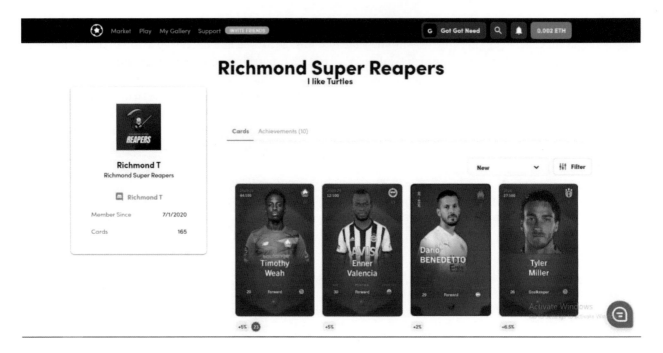

So now we have seen everything about that individual cards background on Sorare, are you ready to buy? If you are anything like me, you'll want to do a bit more research – you guessed it… Sorare Data.

Head to Sorare Data and enter the players name into the search bar:

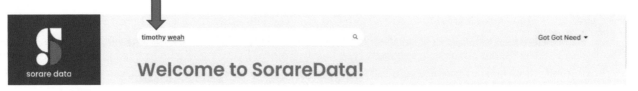

You will bring up the players profile page and we can see the average sale costs for the card; here we can see that Weah's average sale price for a Rare card is 0.095 Eth, the average sale price for the last 3 days is 0.109 Eth. Sorare Data is stating that the current best market offer is 0.099 but having checked Sorare this is an offer that was purchased within the last few hours and is yet to update on the Blockchain hence a slight lag in the update.

Scroll further down the page and we have a breakdown on the sales, I am interested in sales within the last 3 days. I can see that there have been 4 sales within the last 3 days, there was 1 auction which went for 0.105 Eth and there were 3 sales between managers ranging between 0.100-0.122 Eth. The card that we were looking at on the Transfer Market was for sale at 0.120 Eth so I would say that is a fair price going by recent sales alone.

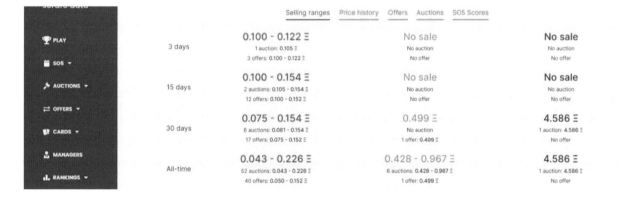

Other considerations to be made at this point before hitting that buy button: -

- Cost of Eth: The Eth to fiat price can be volatile at times to say the least, it has been known to jump around +/- 30% within a 24-hour period so your 0.120 offer on one day may be worth significantly more or less the next day, it is worth bearing this in mind when comparing the Eth value of players. As previously mentioned, I would recommend going through the fiat prices on the Sorare website itself and noting recent sales.

- News on injuries/ transfers/ suspensions: A player's price can significantly fall if they get a bad injury so that 0.120 could halve if they do their ACL and are ruled out for a season, check the player's status before every purchase.

- Fixtures: Check to see if the players season has finished or has come to a long break, this could cause a player's price to drop as other managers move their money into active players.

- Card's bonus level: Less significant than the above but something to consider especially as Sorare becomes more established but we will start to find that some player's cards have a much higher bonus than others and this will in turn give those cards more value, when assessing cards prices make sure to check what bonus level they have and if this is a determining factor.

Obviously, all the above are important aspects to be cautious of when buying but they also present great opportunities also to savvy managers who are willing to pick up deals on out of favour players and look to profit when they do eventually come back into demand.

Assuming you've now done your price checking and due diligence on a player you'll probably have reached 1 of 3 conclusions: deal, no deal or negotiate where Sorare's 'Direct Offers' feature come into play.

Just Collecting!

As you begin to familiarise yourself with the market and selection of cards on offer you will become aware of certain cards which are desired not for their in-game utility but instead for other qualities that can be attributed to a regular collectible market.

There are cards with various misprints such as incorrect names, misspellings, wrong photos or team badges. Then there are the cards which are for fan's favourite players that may have a diminished use within S05 tournaments.

Will there be a market for these cards later down the line? It is rather speculative but something that goes on with many other collectible markets – in January 2021, a Mickey Mantle baseball card sold for $5.2 million, could this be what's to come with our digital Sorare cards in years to come?

Direct Offers

We've found a player that we want to add to our gallery but no cards at the right price, we have three options:

1.   Send a direct offer to a manager from a card's profile
2.   Create a direct offer to a manager from the direct offers screen
3.   Approach managers directly on Discord/ social media

First let's go through how each of the above is done and then we can look at tactics for identifying cards or deals.

1.   **Send a direct offer to a manager from a card's profile**

Start by searching the player you want on Sorare and bringing up all of those cards, you can then order those cards into lowest price to highest. You have the ability to make a direct offer on every one of these cards.

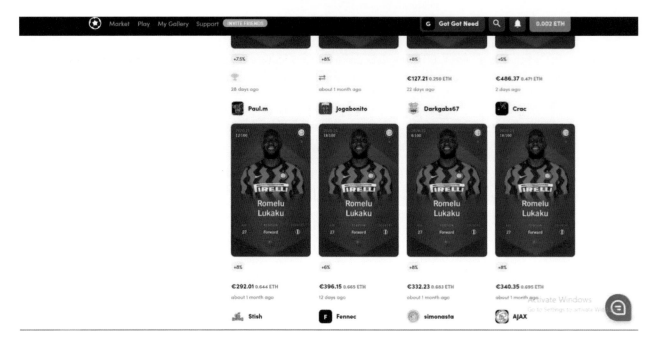

Click on one of the cards to bring up its details, you can see the button marked 'Make Direct Offer', click this to bring up offer screen.

From here we can propose our offer to the manager for their card, enter the Eth or Fiat figure you have in mind and click send. Please note that you will need to have the Eth value sitting in your wallet in order to make the offer, the Eth will then be taken from your wallet to sit in a holding account until the other manager responds.

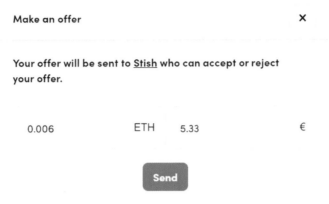

Once you have made an offer to the owner they will receive an email notifying them of the action, they will then be able to accept or decline. The Eth you have offered will continue to sit in holding until the manager responds. You are able to view all your offers by highlighting your name in the header bar and selecting 'Direct Offers'. If you wish to cancel any offers, click on the 'X' under Status.

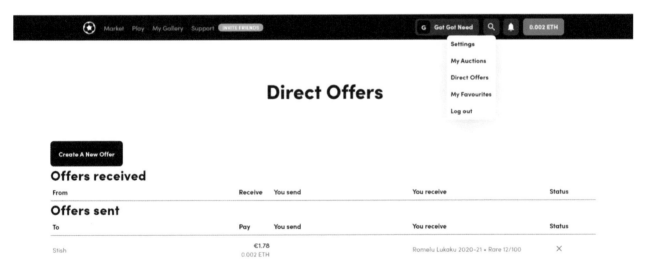

(By the way – that wasn't a serious offer of Lukaku for 0.002 Eth, that's all I had in the account at the time of writing this book!)

2. Create a direct offer to a manager from the Direct Offers screen

There is also a facility for packaging an offer directly to a manager that consists of cards and Eth in exchange for other cards, this can lead to some very creative offers that involve multiple cards in exchange for 1 really desirable card. For this method you will need to have already identified a manager you want to do a deal with.

You can find this feature by heading to the Direct Offers page and clicking on the 'Create A New Offer' button

You will then need to search Sorare for the manager you wish to trade with, enter the managers name on the search bar and press next.

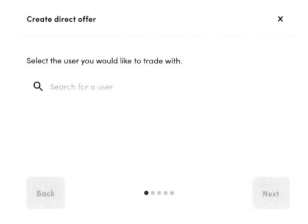

You will then be asked: -
1) How much Eth, if any, you wish to send the manager
2) What cards, if any, you wish to send the manager
3) What cards you wish to receive in return

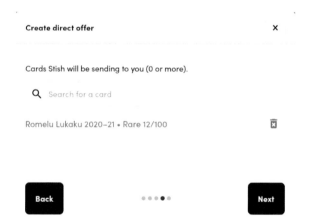

Once you have completed creating the deal you will need to review the offer, if it is all correct you can press 'Submit'. The offer will then appear in your Direct Offers page where you can cancel it any time.

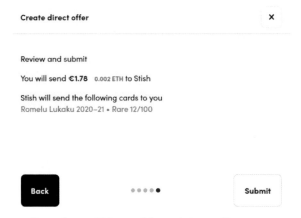

3. Approach managers directly on Discord/ social media

I personally love this element of Sorare, I have connected with a lot of different people from various countries and walks of life after originally getting in touch to do deals on cards.

As we've discussed previously in the book, Discord is a focal point of the Sorare community, and we are able to message the majority of managers using the app to negotiate.

When you have found a card you wish to buy go into its profile to see who the owner is, click on their name to go through to their gallery.

Got Got Need by Daniel Higgs

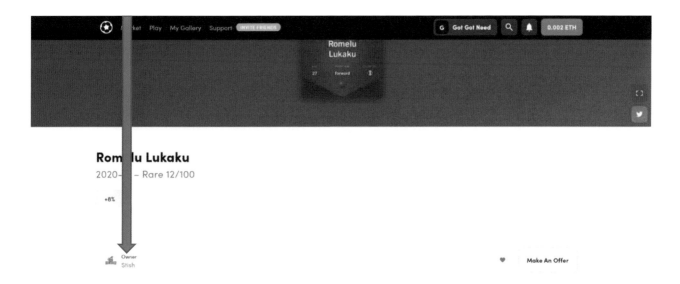

Rome lu Lukaku
2020- – Rare 12/100

+8%

Owner
Stish

♥ Make An Offer

Now we are on the owner's gallery we can view their Discord name, make a note of this and head over to Discord. If the manager is not on Discord, there will be no visible name.

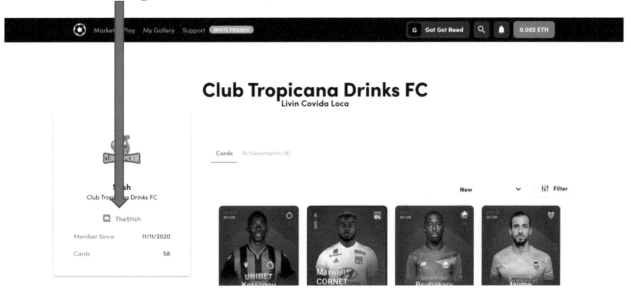

Club Tropicana Drinks FC
Livin Covida Loca

Cards   Achievements (8)

New   ∨   ↖↑↓ Filter

St sh
Club Trop na Drinks FC

💬 TheStish

Member Since   11/11/2020
Cards   58

Once you are on Discord go to the home button in the top left hand corner

From the home screen you can then click on the search bar that says 'Find or start a conversation', this will bring up a search pop up screen.

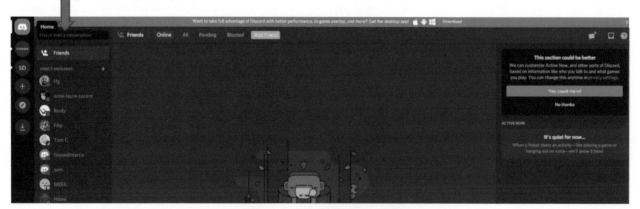

You can now type in the owner's name that you took a note of earlier and enter in this search bar, their name will appear to be selected

A chat screen will now open with the owner and you can begin to open dialogue with them and begin your negotiations – remember to be nice!

Looking for Bargains

Ultimately everyone will value players in their own way and cards are worth whatever someone is willing to pay for them but when it comes to buying and building your gallery there are various methods you can adopt to try and seek out the best deals.

Some managers have finessed their own tactics of acquiring bargains and make a tidy profit from flipping players. Below are some ideas you may want to test and adapt to add players whilst not busting the bank

- Target unwanted gameweek rewards – When managers receive their rewards there are inevitably a few that receive duplicates or card that don't suit their galleries and would rather have a quick sell to get the Eth in their account ready to spend on the market, this can present a great opportunity to pick up some bargains. One man's trash is another man's treasure and all that!

- Buy injured players – As we know when player's sustain injuries their prices tend to drop as owners look to sell them off quickly to cash in and move to other prospects, maybe you have the patience to stash players away until they return from injury or maybe you have more information than others that they will return sooner than expected and can get ahead of the crowd?

- Buy out of season players – Similar to buying injured players; when a season comes to an end or to a winter break you will probably see a pattern in the market where owners look to offload their players and there can be plenty of bargains to be found.

- Transfer targets – One of my favourites, if you think you have some reliable sources or are good at obtaining breaking transfer news before others then you can use this to your advantage. A player moving from a Challenger Europe team to a Champion Europe team will usually increase in value, if you can get there first you can pick up some nice profit.

- Late night/ early morning auctions – You'll often find that auctions which finish in the early morning (1-5am) tend to go for a cheaper price than the prime-time auctions, if you are willing to stay up then you might pick up a deal that could easily be flipped the next day for more money.

Obviously all the above have their risks and challenges so approach with caution and never spend more money than you are comfortable losing.

Selling

There are various reasons you may choose to sell a player – unwanted reward, not scoring great, has signed for a team that isn't metric friendly, whatever the reason the method of putting you player on the market is very simple.

All cards can be sold except for Commons, once a card has been listed it will be on the Transfer Market for 48 hours. Players you have listed can still be used in gameweeks; if you have a listed player in a gameweek team and they sell during that gameweek they will still earn you points. If you have a listed player in a forthcoming gameweek line-up and the card is sold before the gameweek locks in, you will receive an email and in-game notification that your line-up requires attention.

To list a player head over to your gallery and select the card you wish to sell. Once on the card's profile click the button marked 'Sell'.

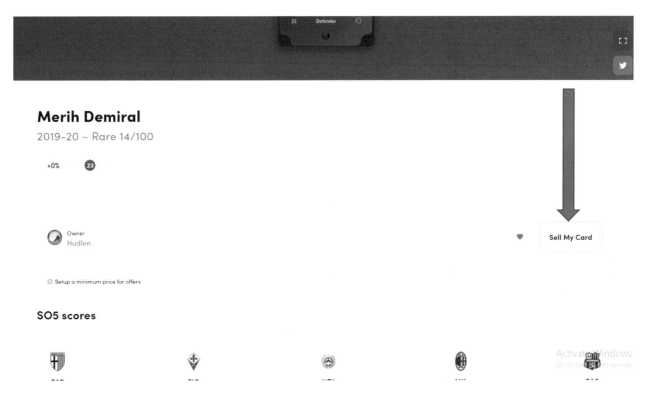

A pop-up screen will then appear prompting you to enter your desired sales figure in either Eth or fiat; at what price you market your card will depend on a number of factors, you may choose to use the methods of valuing that we previously looked at in the book checking Sorare Data and previous recent sales on the Sorare site itself or you may be selling in prospect of the card's price rising due to good performance or a favourable transfer and in these circumstances you will need to use your own judgement perhaps basing off similar players or pure projection.

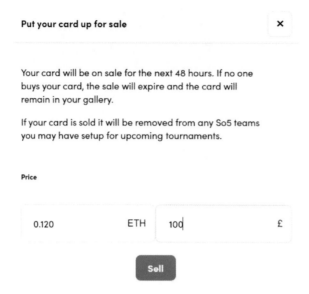

Once you are ready to confirm your sales price press the blue button marked 'Sell', your card will now enter the Transfer Market for 48 hours.

You can view all your cards for sale by selecting the 'My Auction' page under your name then scrolling down to 'Cards You Are Selling'. If you wish to cancel any of your sales hit the 'Cancel Sale' button

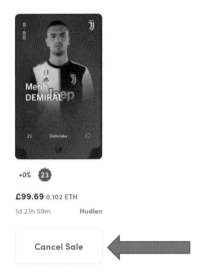

£99.69 0.102 ETH

1d 23h 59m   Hudlen

Cancel Sale

Receiving Direct Offers

If you receive a direct offer from another manager you will receive an email alert and a notification symbol will pop up in your home screen. To access your direct offer select 'Direct Offers' under your name. Then scroll down to 'Offers received'.

You have three options at this point under 'Status': -

- Accept (Tick) – This confirms the proposed offer and the transfer will proceed.
- Decline (Cross) – This rejects the proposed offer and transfer will be cancelled.
- Block (No Entry) – This option is best reserved if you receive multiple, spam type offers from a particular manager or someone that becomes abusive on Discord etc.

Once you have made a sale the player will go into transfer and the Eth will start to make its way over to your wallet, the transaction period can take a variable amount of time from instantaneous to a few hours and usually depends on how busy the blockchain is.

XP when Transferring Players

When a player card is transferred between managers it will incur a reduction of 50% to its XP, this is to dissuade managers from continually loaning cards between themselves to gain unfair advantages over others.

It is the XP which is reduced and not the level bonus itself. If you refer to the XP progression chart on page 13 you will see that if a level 20 card has its XP reduced by 50% it will go to level 15.

This is something to consider when buying should a cards bonus level be taken into consideration.

11
WHAT NEXT?

I hope you've found the guide helpful and it gives you some ideas going forward. I'm sure at this point you are equally excited about what's to come in the future as Sorare acquires more teams, more leagues and the global community grows; just whilst writing this book SorareData have begun hosting knock-out cups and 11-a-side leagues for your Sorare cards and other independent developers are working on other ideas to utilise your cards– the possibilities are endless, and I feel we are at the start of something amazing.

Still have questions or seeking guidance? No problem feel free to contact me on twitter @hudlen_ my DMs are open, alternatively, and as I've mentioned before the Sorare community is a really co-operative bunch, something I believe is a result of the negotiation element within the game, so don't hesitate in reaching out.

I've listed below some really useful community members and resources that will help you on your journey:

- Quinny's YouTube channel http://youtube.com/c/Quinny101 - Loads of helpful tutorials and does a team selection each gameweek which can be great for getting a few ideas and player updates.
- Hibee and YNWA's weekly podcast www.thesorarepodcast.com – Great content and really interesting guests each week, can be a great idea going back through the old episodes to listen to how the platform has grown in a short space of time.
- Follow @SorareHub on twitter as they provide some neat breakdowns including how competitive each of the S05s currently are which can help your decision making in targeting tournaments.
- Getting up to date team and player information for some of the S05s can be difficult, in particular Asia which is perhaps affected by the language barrier and not quite having the same football obsessed culture as Europe, specialist information services will be in demand and one

such established resource is @SorareJapan on twitter who gives updates but also has a subscription service making sure you get the news first.

- @SorareInfo (www.sorareinfo.substack.com/p/coming-soon) provide users looking to build teams on a budget with scouting information for players at bargain prices, they have a proven track record for finding value and are worth following on twitter and signing up to their newsletter.

Good luck with your Sorare journey, see you at the S05s!

Printed in Great Britain
by Amazon

12865845R00063